CR⌀P CIF
2015

Extraterrestrial Cosmology

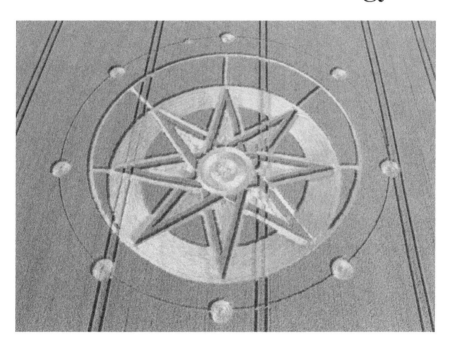

ANDREW G FREW

Contents

Dedication

This book is dedicated to Lucy a four year old who gave us a different perspective on the shapes in the Crop Circles by naming them. Also I have felt deep inside while interpreting Crop Circles that I am not being taught by alien adults but by the alien children. Since, the future belongs to our children this book is so, dedicated.

Note from Author

Like most people I have never really paid much attention to Crop Circles, they have just seemed to me to be harmless phenomena that the farmers of the fields were singularly annoyed about. The kind of groups that gathered around these Crop Circles seemed to me to be the New Age types, who advocated a new way of living. At first these Crop Circle designs were just circles, hence the name they have been given and they all just seemed perpetrated, after all anybody could make a circle in a field and claim it made by aliens! I was very skeptical of Crop Circles and when news reports broke that they were claimed to be made by men as a UFO hoax I left the whole idea of any serious study of them in the proverbial bin. But since those early days of Crop Circle formations, thirty years ago, I have witnessed a gradual complexity in them that has stunned the imagination to such an extent of concluding that these geometrical patterns are so complex humans have not that ability to make them. I was left with an enigma, what do they mean, what are they telling us, is any language used or knowledge contained within them. This book is the third in a series into Crop Circles showing my findings.

Introduction

In this work we are going to explore the hidden knowledge behind Crop Circles indeed the greatest phenomenon of the millennia. I have taken all the documented sightings of Crop Circles archived from the year 2015 and analysed their meaning giving a photo as it appeared alongside a graphic detail and a cosmic presentation of the knowledge contained within the message from the Crop Circle. It is for the reader to decide whether my analysis is correct. I know there are skeptics to this phenomenon who believe this is a human prank, but for my study I have only included Crop Circles that are considered genuine. This process is done by studying the broken stems of the plant. It has been found those stem nodes that have undergone internal combustion are a sure sign of a genuine made natural Crop Circle without human contamination. Below is given the examination of the plant within the Crop Circle after formation.

The normal, how the plant appears, the bent due to human activity and the blown, the sign that a genuine Crop Circle has formed. The blown reveals that the stem has combusted within its node not externally but internally heated so as the stem can lay in formation. Very much akin to the energy process of a microwave oven that uses microwaves to heat the food internally. Once heated the plant lays in patterns in the field, by a process not known but likely to be by electromagnetic fields surrounding the process guided to form the design of the Crop Circle, a technology not yet been developed.

Intricate pattern contained within a Crop Circle.

A magnetic compass placed within a recently formed Crop Circle is shown to act wildly, showing an erratic Electro Magnetic field. The question, what makes Crop Circles? If it is not humanly made then is it naturally formed or is it of an alien intelligence? Who or what makes Crop Circles? The natural answer would be naturally made but because of their intricate intelligent designs, it doubtful. Which seems to lead us to the conclusion extraterrestrial life is the instigator, of these formations. We have film showing the making of one of these Crop Circles and it shows that round orbs of light are responsible. They are possibly an alien drone of some sought.

These balls of light move extremely fast and the Crop Circle above was formed within minutes. We do not know the means of their energy it can only be speculation, but as soon as they have formed the Crop Circle they just as soon disappear only to return to design more. These orbs seem to concentrate their work on ancient sites.

Fig a. Two orbs of light filmed above field.

Fig b. Indentations appear in the field.

Fig c. The outline of a Crop Circle can be seen forming.

A couple of lights

Stonehenge has seen many Crop Circles.

The vast array of shapes, geometrical patterns and the enormity of the size of these Crop Circles seem to boggle the mind they seem at first to only have the language of metaphor which anybody with an imaginative mind could interpret with many tongues as many ideas, which those listening take as a pinch of salt. I quite frankly steered away from publishing this kind of book, I felt others had covered the phenomena quite adequately but I was left with the feeling that Crop Circles were and are still a mystery. I wanted to know more what these great metaphors of what appeared to be of extraterrestrial origin had to really say. Those that claimed to be able to read them seemed to me the types that could explain the same kind of esoteric art emanating from the modern art museums.

In researching this Crop Circle activity I have noticed a change in their frequency in 2015. The formations had their climax in the last decade and looking over the Crop Circle formations in 2015, gone are the vast, jaw dropping, complicated geometrical patterns of former years that just dazzled the mind. But instead were replaced with uncomplicated displays, with simpler patterns of the eighties. A reappraisal moment perhaps I see there is a noticeable return to a simpler mode of expression perhaps we of this generation might interpret. This was the catalyst for this work to try to understand these simpler shapes to shed light on these simpler formations. This enabled me to take a closer look at the whole and find that through design they contained fundamental information pertaining to our earth. I needed a means to interpret this I believe extraterrestrial message I found it in the pseudo science that traced its roots all the way back to Babylon, Egypt, Greece and Rome. The science of astrology the language of the stars mans first attempt to understand the universe.

With each, new crop materialization I drew up an astrological chart showing the positions of the planets, the Sun and Moon on the day that the formation in the fields was discovered. The areas these circles mostly appeared were found to be in the Netherlands and in Wiltshire, Warwickshire, Essex and other sites in England. It has to be noted that over 90% of these crop formations occur in these locations. We do not know why this is the case but these places have historical roots of ancients mounds and temples that are the oldest in the world. Also because of the proliferation of wheat, barley, oilseed rape and grass grown in these areas, it might be the type of canvas the creators of these Crop Circles need, for their technology to reproduce them. For instance, if they were done in the sand surrounding the pyramid in Egypt for instance they would not remain long before blown away, before people had a chance to examine them indeed that appears to be their objective for creation. For us as a race to recognize what the most advanced civilizations in the universe have to tell us about our own world and our place in it to help us depart from the eve of our own destruction by working along with the natural forces that are contained in the universe that pertain to our very survival on this our planet earth. Those scoffing the stars can have any influence on us will necessary bear in mind it is the most advanced civilizations in the universe that reveal to us this fact, too work with the natural forces around us to enable us to expand our spiritual consciousness to think, what have people to gain if they dead have lost the means of obtaining to their true self.

With detrimental human activity, resulting environmental damage, the loss of natural habitats and species all a ruination to our planet. The hope seems impossible but our children are our hope and it is only through them our planet secured, it after all belongs to them. The hopelessness of the last generation need not be visited on them they have the means to choose to make a choice. Sadly, and all too evidently we like sheep rather not make. But in time circumstances will be forced upon us. They the creators of these circles that you will find in this small book are a reflection of that hope that their message will be understood that we too are all children of the stars.

Author

CHAPTER ONE

CROP CIRCLES IN APRIL 2015

We are going to examine chronologically those Crop Circles that appeared in 2015. Those reported by people to Crop Circle Center which is the largest internet data base site for logging Crop Circles. Their data goes back years. But we shall be concentrating on just the one year, to try and make some sense out of the phenomena. I understand some readers will be new to this but we are dealing with cosmic patterns revealed in our solar system. These patterns are well known to those who have studied the ancient science of astrology. The pseudo-science that states what happens above shall have its consequence below on this our earth. This appears to be what the makers of the Crop Circles are revealing to us that we are interconnected through the planetary dynamics of our solar system.

We begin with the first reported sighting of a Crop Circle in 2015. Often they appear in early March or April and finish in September. The first Crop Circle appeared in Wiltshire, a very simple one it just the design of a circle, like the early Crop Circle designs in the 80's. They progressively get more complicated as we progress through the year. We are led very slowly like a child in kinder garden to learn the fundamentals first the A,B,C of this knowledge.

When we look to the sky the first design we see is a circle, the sun or Moon, the stars, the planets through a telescope. Thus the circle tells us we are to look at an orb in the sky, which orb will become clear as we progress with this knowledge. There is going to appear symbols that the reader may find strange but it is the way this hidden knowledge is presented. I will explain latter as we progress.

WILTSHIRE 9TH APRIL 2015

c
london, UK
Apr 9 2015
12:00:00 PM BST

Symbols of the Planets and Signs

☉ = Sun	♄ = Saturn	♈ = Aries	♎ = Libra
☽ = Moon	♅ = Uranus	♉ = Taurus	♏ = Scorpio
☿ = Mercury	♆ = Neptune	♊ = Gemini	♐ = Sagittarius
♀ = Venus	♇ = Pluto	♋ = Cancer	♑ = Capricorn
♂ = Mars	☊ = N. Node	♌ = Leo	♒ = Aquarius
♃ = Jupiter	⚕ = Retrograde	♍ = Virgo	♓ = Pisces

Angles are the dynamics between planets and the Sun and Moon in the sky. These are divided into the semi-sextile 30 degrees, the sextile 60 degrees, the square 90 degrees, the trine 120 degrees and the opposition 180 degrees. The orb angles as seen from the Earth.

The above chart shows the planetary positions and their angles on the 9th April 2015. We are told to look at the smaller orb that is in a circle. This orb is connected to another orb, but what orbs are they?

The Crop Circles that follow provide us with our answers.

GLOUCESTERSHIRE 19TH APRIL 2015

The disc pertaining to the sun contains four shapes these are the surrounding orbs Mars, Mercury, Moon and Uranus in the heavens. There are 30 shapes surrounding the disc and four inside shapes. In subtraction equals 26 degrees, the spatial separation of the planets.

THE NETHERLANDS 28TH APRIL 2015

Symbols of the Planets and Signs			
☉ = Sun	♄ = Saturn	♈ = Aries	♎ = Libra
☽ = Moon	♅ = Uranus	♉ = Taurus	♏ = Scorpio
☿ = Mercury	♆ = Neptune	♊ = Gemini	♐ = Sagittarius
♀ = Venus	♇ = Pluto	♋ = Cancer	♑ = Capricorn
♂ = Mars	☊ = N. Node	♌ = Leo	♒ = Aquarius
♃ = Jupiter	☋ = Retrograde	♍ = Virgo	♓ = Pisces

In this Crop Circle formation we have a worm hole or black hole at the position of Saturn at 3 degrees Sagittarius affecting all planets. We are to look at this area in order to understand the next graphic.

CHAPTER TWO

CROP CIRCLES IN MAY 2015

THE NETHERLANDS 6TH MAY 2015

Symbols of the Planets and Signs			
☉ = Sun	♄ = Saturn	♈ = Aries	♎ = Libra
☽ = Moon	♅ = Uranus	♉ = Taurus	♏ = Scorpio
☿ = Mercury	♆ = Neptune	♊ = Gemini	♐ = Sagittarius
♀ = Venus	♇ = Pluto	♋ = Cancer	♑ = Capricorn
♂ = Mars	☊ = N. Node	♌ = Leo	♒ = Aquarius
♃ = Jupiter	℞ = Retrograde	♍ = Virgo	♓ = Pisces

In the Crop Circle we see the Moon eclipses a planet. The Moon at 12 degrees Sagittarius makes a planetary transit over Saturn at 02 degrees Sagittarius. The small orb next to it is Pluto at 15 degrees Capricorn followed by Neptune at 9 degrees Pisces then Uranus at 18 degrees Aries then Sun at 15 degrees Taurus then in the orbit connecting Uranus is Mercury at 6 degrees Gemini. Both Uranus and Mercury are dynamic octaves. The inner orbit we have Mars at 25 degrees Taurus followed by Venus at 28 degrees Gemini and finally Jupiter at 13 degrees Leo.

NETHERLANDS 19TH MAY 2015

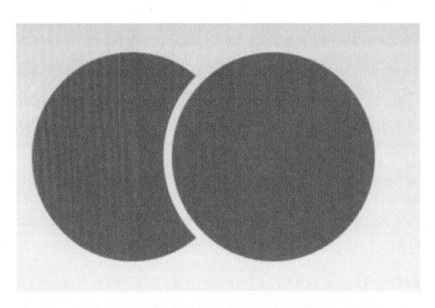

A PASSING TRANSIT OF ORBS

A Crop Circle revealing the passing transit of orbs that takes place 19th May between the Moon and Mercury at 13/14 degrees Gemini.

NETHERLANDS 19TH MAY 2015

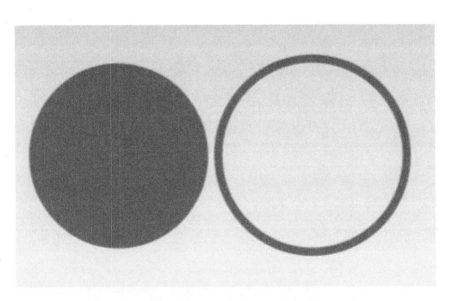

A PASSING TRANSIT OF ORBS

Symbols of the Planets and Signs			
☉ = Sun	♄ = Saturn	♈ = Aries	♎ = Libra
☽ = Moon	♅ = Uranus	♉ = Taurus	♏ = Scorpio
☿ = Mercury	♆ = Neptune	♊ = Gemini	♐ = Sagittarius
♀ = Venus	♇ = Pluto	♋ = Cancer	♑ = Capricorn
♂ = Mars	☊ = N. Node	♌ = Leo	♒ = Aquarius
♃ = Jupiter	↺ = Retrograde	♍ = Virgo	♓ = Pisces

A Crop Circle revealing the passing transit of orbs that takes place 19th May between the Moon and Mercury at 13/14 degrees Gemini.

WILTSHIRE 24TH MAY 2015

A Crop Circle is showing the angles between planets not making a perfect geometrical shape shown by an off placement of one point.

DORSET 30TH MAY 2015

Four inner quadrants surrounded by four circles the number eight. The moon at 0 degrees Scorpio enters the eight sign of the Zodiac.

CHAPTER THREE

CROP CIRCLES IN JUNE 2015

THE NETHERLANDS 4TH JUNE 2015

Symbols of the Planets and Signs

☉ = Sun	♄ = Saturn	♈ = Aries	♎ = Libra
☽ = Moon	♅ = Uranus	♉ = Taurus	♏ = Scorpio
☿ = Mercury	♆ = Neptune	♊ = Gemini	♐ = Sagittarius
♀ = Venus	♇ = Pluto	♋ = Cancer	♑ = Capricorn
♂ = Mars	☊ = N. Node	♌ = Leo	♒ = Aquarius
♃ = Jupiter	↾ = Retrograde	♍ = Virgo	♓ = Pisces

The Crop Circle graphic directs us towards Venus and Mars to the left of sun and to the planets Mercury and Uranus to the suns right.

WILTSHIRE 9TH JUNE 2015

SPATIAL HOLE

THE NETHERLANDS 9TH JUNE 2015

SPATIAL WORM

WILTSHIRE 15TH JUNE 2015

LOCATION OF WORMHOLE

Symbols of the Planets and Signs			
☉ = Sun	♄ = Saturn	♈ = Aries	♎ = Libra
☽ = Moon	⛢ = Uranus	♉ = Taurus	♏ = Scorpio
☿ = Mercury	♆ = Neptune	♊ = Gemini	♐ = Sagittarius
♀ = Venus	♇ = Pluto	♋ = Cancer	♑ = Capricorn
♂ = Mars	☊ = N. Node	♌ = Leo	♒ = Aquarius
♃ = Jupiter	℞ = Retrograde	♍ = Virgo	♓ = Pisces

We are directed by the Crop Circle towards the position of a space wormhole positioned on the mid heaven point M.C. at 10 degrees Gemini the location of an arrival by Extraterrestrials. A wormhole can be visualized as a tunnel with two ends, each at separate points in space time (i.e., different locations and/or different points of time), or by a transcendental bijection of the space time continuum.

Wormholes are consistent with the general theory of relativity, but whether wormholes actually exists remains to be seen.

Wormhole Is Best Bet for Time Machine, Astrophysicist Says

Traveling forward in time is an uncontroversial possibility, according to Einstein's theory. In fact, physicists have been able to send tiny particles called muons, which are similar to electrons, forward in time by manipulating the gravity around them. That's not to say the technology for sending humans 100 years into the future will be available anytime soon, though.

Time travel to the past, however, is even less understood. Still, astrophysicist Eric W. Davis, of the Earth Tech International Institute for Advanced Studies at Austin, argues that it's possible. All you need, he says, is a wormhole, which is a theoretical passageway through space-time that is predicted by relativity.

"You can go into the future or into the past using traversable wormholes," Davis told Live Science.

Wormholes have never been proven to exist, and if they are ever found, they are likely to be so tiny that a person couldn't fit inside, never mind a spaceship.

Even so, Davis' paper, published in July 2013 in the American Institute of Aeronautics and Astronautics' journal, addresses time machines and the possibility that a wormhole could become, or be used as, a means for traveling backward in time.

Both general-relativity theory and quantum theory appear to offer several possibilities for traveling along what physicists call a "closed, timelike curve," or a path that cuts through time and space — essentially, a time machine.

In fact, Davis said, scientists' current understanding of the laws of physics "are infested with time machines whereby there are numerous space-time geometry solutions that exhibit time travel and/or have the properties of time machines."

A wormhole would allow a ship, for instance, to travel from one point to another faster than the speed of light — sort of. That's because the ship would arrive at its destination sooner than a beam of light would, by taking a shortcut through space-time via the wormhole. That way, the vehicle doesn't actually break the rule of the so-called universal speed limit — the speed of light — because the ship never actually travels at a speed faster than light.

Theoretically, a wormhole could be used to cut not just through space, but through time as well.

"Time machines are unavoidable in our physical dimensional space-time," David wrote in his paper. "Traversable wormholes imply time machines, and [the prediction of wormholes] spawned a number of follow-on research efforts on time machines."

However, Davis added, turning a wormhole into a time machine won't be easy. "It would take a Herculean effort to turn a wormhole into a time machine. It's going to be tough enough to pull off a wormhole," he told Live Science.

That's because once a wormhole is created, one or both ends of it would need to be accelerated through time to the desired position, according to general relativity theory.

Live Science

SURREY 16TH JUNE 2015

16 PYRAMID SYMBOLS

WILTSHIRE 16TH JUNE 2015

WILTSHIRE 19TH JUNE 2015

C
london, UK
Jun 19 2015
12:00:00 PM BST

Symbols of the Planets and Signs			
☉ = Sun	♄ = Saturn	♈ = Aries	♎ = Libra
☽ = Moon	♅ = Uranus	♉ = Taurus	♏ = Scorpio
☿ = Mercury	♆ = Neptune	♊ = Gemini	♐ = Sagittarius
♀ = Venus	♇ = Pluto	♋ = Cancer	♑ = Capricorn
♂ = Mars	☊ = N. Node	♌ = Leo	♒ = Aquarius
♃ = Jupiter	℞ = Retrograde	♍ = Virgo	♓ = Pisces

A basic graphic of the four co ordinates the Mid-heaven point, I.C, ASC and DSC.

WILTSHIRE 21ST JUNE 2015

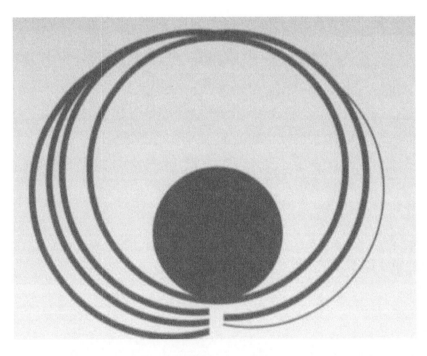

THE TRANSIT OF THE SUN BETWEEN SIGNS

Symbols of the Planets and Signs			
☉ = Sun	♄ = Saturn	♈ = Aries	♎ = Libra
☽ = Moon	♅ = Uranus	♉ = Taurus	♏ = Scorpio
☿ = Mercury	♆ = Neptune	♊ = Gemini	♐ = Sagittarius
♀ = Venus	♇ = Pluto	♋ = Cancer	♑ = Capricorn
♂ = Mars	☊ = N. Node	♌ = Leo	♒ = Aquarius
♃ = Jupiter	℞ = Retrograde	♍ = Virgo	♓ = Pisces

The Crop Circle break shows the transit of the sun over the signs Gemini and Cancer the disc representing the suns position in the heavens at 29 degrees Gemini on the verge of entering into Cancer.

On the left side three cut circles representing 3 degrees for Mars at 27 degrees Gemini to enter Cancer and on the right side one cut circle representing the 1 degree for the sun at 29 degrees Gemini to enter Cancer.

WILTSHIRE 22ND JUNE 2015

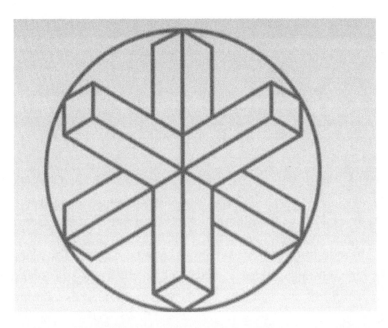

TWELVE SIDES TWELVE SIGNS OF THE ZODIAC

THE NUMBER TWELVE

SOMERSET 22ND JUNE 2015

A MAZE

SUN IN CANCER IS ASSOCIATED WITH MEMORY

WILTSHIRE 23RD JUNE 2015

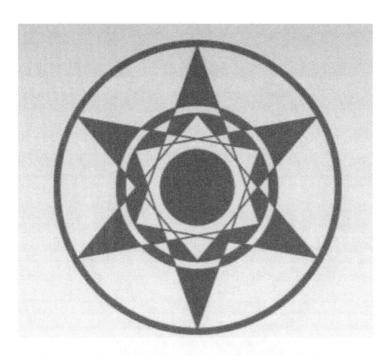

THE NUMBER SIX THE HEXAGON

AS ABOVE, SO BELOW

ITALY 23RD JUNE 2015

ASCII-based standard character encodings

THE NUMBER EIGHT

STONEHENGE WILTSHIRE 24TH JUNE 2015

THE MOON THE GOVENOR OF CANCER

THE NUMBER FOUR

WILTSHIRE 29TH JUNE 2015

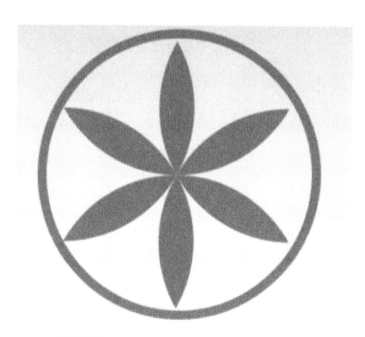

THE NUMBER SIX THE HEXAGON

AS ABOVE, SO BELOW

CHAPTER FOUR

CROP CIRCLES IN JULY 2015

THE NETHERLANDS 4TH JULY 2015

THE EGYPTIAN ANKH AND TWO ORBS

Symbols of the Planets and Signs

☉ = Sun	♄ = Saturn	♈ = Aries	♎ = Libra
☽ = Moon	♅ = Uranus	♉ = Taurus	♏ = Scorpio
☿ = Mercury	♆ = Neptune	♊ = Gemini	♐ = Sagittarius
♀ = Venus	♇ = Pluto	♋ = Cancer	♑ = Capricorn
♂ = Mars	☊ = N. Node	♌ = Leo	♒ = Aquarius
♃ = Jupiter	℞ = Retrograde	♍ = Virgo	♓ = Pisces

Nfr-Ka Ma'at   Heru Djeden Ma'at Aten-Ra

The Egyptian Ankh the symbol of life in the Egyptian underworld is represented here by Pluto the god of the underworld positioned at 14 degrees Capricorn while the two orbs represent the sun and Mars positioned opposite Pluto in the skies as seen from the earth.

WILTSHIRE 6TH JULY 2015

THE NUMBER FIVE

The Crop Circle shows two groups of orbs sun/Mars in opposition
180 degrees and Moon/Neptune in sextile 60 degrees that connect
with the planet Pluto at 14 degrees Capricorn.

WILTSHIRE 9TH JULY 2015

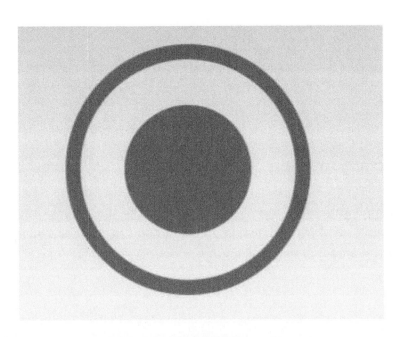

MARS AT 9 DEGREES CANCER

THE NUMBER NINE

WILTSHIRE 9TH JULY 2015

THE MOON TRANSITS URANUS

THE NUMBER FOUR

WILTSHIRE 14TH JULY 2015

A RABBIT BETWEEN THREE ORBS

C
london, UK
Jul 14 2015
12:00:00 PM BST

Three orbs are identified in the Crop Circle primarily the sun at 21 degrees Cancer, Mars at 13 degrees Cancer and Mercury at 10 degrees Cancer. All three orbs in opposition to Pluto at 14 degrees Capricorn a configuration symbolic of the movement of the rabbit.

OXFORDSHIRE 15TH JULY 2015

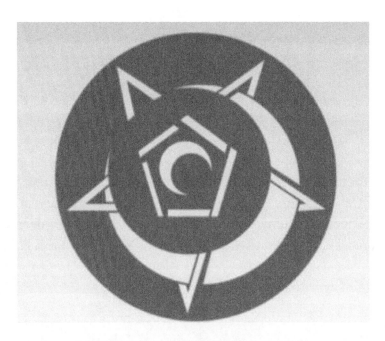

MOON AT 15 DEGREES CANCER

A Crop Circle pentagram formed from the position of the transiting Moon these are the angle dynamics that are formed in the heavens.

OXFORDSHIRE 15TH JULY 2015

PLUTO OPPOSITE THE MOON

THE NETHERLANDS 15TH JULY 2015

30 CIRCLES EQUATING TO 30 DEGREES THAT MAKE UP
ONE OF THE SIGNS (SEE INSIGNIA)

WARWICKSHIRE 19TH JULY 2015

THE STAR OF BETHLEHEM

Symbols of the Planets and Signs			
☉ = Sun	♄ = Saturn	♈ = Aries	♎ = Libra
☽ = Moon	♅ = Uranus	♉ = Taurus	♏ = Scorpio
☿ = Mercury	♆ = Neptune	♊ = Gemini	♐ = Sagittarius
♀ = Venus	♇ = Pluto	♋ = Cancer	♑ = Capricorn
♂ = Mars	☊ = N. Node	♌ = Leo	♒ = Aquarius
♃ = Jupiter	℞ = Retrograde	♍ = Virgo	♓ = Pisces

A STARLIKE STRUCTURE FORMED BY THE OUTER PLANETS

The dynamics of the angles in the heavens between the orbs form a star ray-like structure which we see represented by the Crop Circle.

The aliens are showing us that the star of Bethlehem was not a star at all but the angular relationships found in the orbs by astrologers. As in the star configuration above we see Venus entering Virgo the sign of the Virgin. The star emanates from Leo the Lion of Judah.

THE STAR OF BETHLEHEM

Now when Jesus was born in Bethlehem of Judea in the days of Herod the king, behold there came wise men from the east to Jerusalem, saying "Where is he that is born King of the Jews? For we have seen his star in the east, and are come to worship him". . . . and lo, the star, which they saw in the east, went before them, till it came and stood over where the young child was. When they saw the star, they rejoiced with exceeding great joy.

Matthew 2: 1-2, 9-10

In the chart above it should be noticed that not one, two or three etc, but all the planets take part in the angular dynamics to form the geometrical pattern of the star, this in itself is a rare star formation.

WILTSHIRE 25TH JULY 2015

AN EGYPTIAN SCARAB OF HORUS

SYMBOL OF HORUS THE SUN GOD

ALIENS ASSOCIATE THE EGYPTIAN HORUS WITH
CHRIST

SURREY 29TH JULY 2015

4+4+1+8+8+8 = 33AD

THE DEATH OF CHRIST

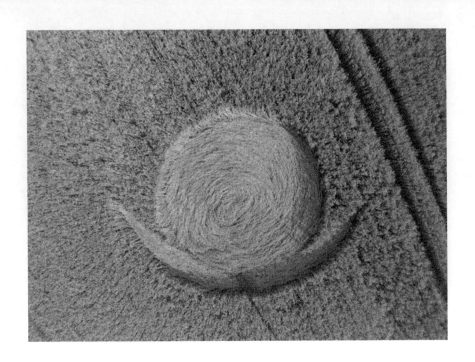

THE NETHERLANDS 31ST JULY 2015

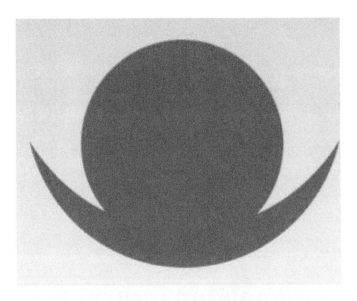

SUN AND MOON AT THE CRUCIFIXION

Symbols of the Planets and Signs			
☉ = Sun	♄ = Saturn	♈ = Aries	♎ = Libra
☽ = Moon	♅ = Uranus	♉ = Taurus	♏ = Scorpio
☿ = Mercury	♆ = Neptune	♊ = Gemini	♐ = Sagittarius
♀ = Venus	♇ = Pluto	♋ = Cancer	♑ = Capricorn
♂ = Mars	☊ = N. Node	♌ = Leo	♒ = Aquarius
♃ = Jupiter	℞ = Retrograde	♍ = Virgo	♓ = Pisces

The sun positioned at 7 degrees Leo is in opposition 180 degrees to the Moon positioned at 7 degrees Aquarius a reference to the sun and Moon at the time of the crucifixion of Christ in the Gospels.

A translation of the Gospel of Luke 23:44-45 in the New American Bible:

"It was now about noon and darkness came over the whole land until three in the afternoon because of an eclipse of the sun."

CHAPTER FIVE

CROP CIRCLES IN AUGUST 2015

WILTSHIRE 4TH AUGUST 2015

THE NUMBER FOUR

WILTSHIRE 8TH AUGUST 2015

FOUR ELEMENTS IN THE TWELVE SIGNS

EARTH, AIR, FIRE, WATER.

WARWICKSHIRE 8TH AUGUST 2015

Symbols of the Planets and Signs			
☉ = Sun	♄ = Saturn	♈ = Aries	♎ = Libra
☽ = Moon	♅ = Uranus	♉ = Taurus	♏ = Scorpio
☿ = Mercury	♆ = Neptune	♊ = Gemini	♐ = Sagittarius
♀ = Venus	♇ = Pluto	♋ = Cancer	♑ = Capricorn
♂ = Mars	☊ = N Node	♌ = Leo	♒ = Aquarius
♃ = Jupiter	⚡ = Retrograde	♍ = Virgo	♓ = Pisces

The Crop Circle designed as a bird is a graphic representation of the dynamics between the planets as displayed on the 8th August a flight of wing from the Saturn and Moon opposition in the Zodiac.

WILTSHIRE 9TH AUGUST 2015

TRANSIT OF MARS

The Crop Circle identifies the location of Mars at 00 degrees Leo.

TELFORD AND WREKIN 10TH AUGUST 2015

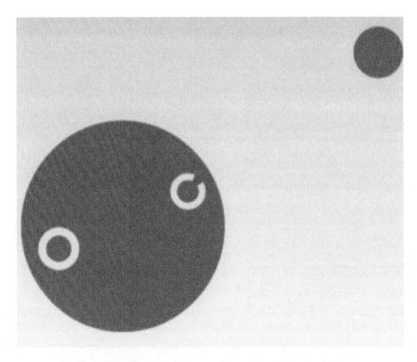

THE ASPECTS FROM THE NORTH NODE

Symbols of the Planets and Signs

☉ = Sun	♄ = Saturn	♈ = Aries	♎ = Libra
☽ = Moon	♅ = Uranus	♉ = Taurus	♏ = Scorpio
☿ = Mercury	♆ = Neptune	♊ = Gemini	♐ = Sagittarius
♀ = Venus	♇ = Pluto	♋ = Cancer	♑ = Capricorn
♂ = Mars	☊ = N. Node	♌ = Leo	♒ = Aquarius
♃ = Jupiter	↑ = Retrograde	♍ = Virgo	♓ = Pisces

A graphical representation of the North Node at 1 degrees Libra squaring 90 degrees Moon at 29 degrees Gemini sextile 60 degrees Saturn at 28 degrees Scorpio.

The **North Node ( )** and South **Node ( )** of the Moon are points that are directly opposite each other. Together, they form the Nodal Axis. They are not planetary bodies; rather, they are mathematical points that take into account the relationship between the Sun, Moon, and Earth at the time of our birth. In astrology, your life purpose is encoded in the **north node** and south **node** of the moon.

WILTSHIRE 19TH AUGUST 2015

The Crop Circle design as a trapezium a graphic representation of
the dynamics between the planets as displayed on the 19th August

THE NETHERLANDS 10TH SEPTEMBER 2015

THE YEAR ENDS WITH THE RETURN OF THE ALIEN TO
HIS HOME THROUGH A WORMHOLE.

It is a law of nature that the microcosm reflects the macrocosm. This is summed up in the Hermetic axiom, 'As above, so below.' Our planetary system consists of one great central fixed star, the Sun, around which the planets revolve in their orbits at varying speeds. From the point of view of an observer standing on one of these planets the Sun will appear to be the moving body and will consequently seem to make a complete circuit of the Zodiac while actually the planet is travelling once around the Sun. This passage, or apparent passage, of the Sun through the twelve signs of the Zodiac is a symbolic equivalent of one whole cycle of experience. Because the aliens are concerned solely with effects on this planet, we on the Earth should base our knowledge on the apparent motion of the Sun and the motion of the planets in relation to our own planet. This is the extraterrestrial knowledge that is imparted to us.

CHAPTER SIX

DO WE HAVE CONTACT

The government of course knows of crop circles and are a mystery to them as to us, but they are wary that the messages sent may transform our society from a material based ego centric selfish world to a new world of equality, sharing and harmoniousness. Have we evidence of true communication, yes. In 1974 a digitally encoded message was beamed from a Puerto Rico radio telescope out into space by a team of U.S. SETI astronomers. It was sent as a digitized code that can be reconstructed into an image directed to any life forms that could receive this message. This image included information about our Earth civilization with data about our human body chemistry, our DNA, our height and appearance, our population numbers, our solar system with our sun, and our means of transmitting messages into space.

Chilbolton Glyph, UK   Arecibo, PR, radio image

August 20, 2001   November 16, 1974

In August of 2001, an answer was returned to us as a Crop Circle for the world to see. It contained similar information to the one we sent out, from a civilization attempting to communicate with us. To do this, they were somehow able to send their message through a means more advanced than any technology we now possess. In their transmission it appears they say they use telepathy to transmit to us.

AUGUST 14, 2001   AUGUST 14, 2002

This crop circle of an ET face is formed next to a microwave station. This is giving us a clue about how to contact them with our technology. According to Palden Jenkins, microwave systems are ideal because they offer superior high-speed wideband links for video and digital telecommunication signals to and from space. This medium provides services such as cellular phones, television programming and emergency services.

The 2002 crop circle of the ET face contains a disc that appears to be the same format as a DVD or a CD-ROM disc when looked at under high magnification. Looking at it, you would see blocks representing digital bits of information. The blocks of information are organized as a spiral. These can be decoded into letters and then words.

Beware the bearers of FALSE gifts & their BROKEN PROMISES.

Much PAIN but still time.

There is GOOD out there.

We Oppose DECEPTION.

Conduit CLOSING (BELL SOUND)

CHAPTER SEVEN

THE CROP CIRCLE GALLERY

Star

Snow globe

Smiley Face

Diamond

A sun with a shell in the middle

Googley eyes

That's actually a snake in a pond

A tiger

Air balloon!

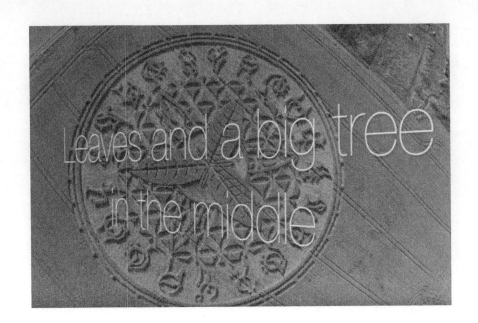

Leaves and a big tree in the middle

A star! With spots

A shepherd

A robots face

Somthing that we put on presents. (a bow)

A hosepipe

Spots everywhere

A flower

APPENDIX

PEOPLES REACTION TO CROP CIRCLES

I'm the journalist who last week exclusively reported Laurance Rockefeller's decision to fund a study of crop circles. My article for the Western Daily Press of Bristol was seized upon by news agencies around the world and I was amazed to see that this patently man-made creation still exerts such a fascinating hold on the gullible. I've studied crop circles for a decade now in the course of my work as a journalist. I like a good mystery as much as the next man, but these circles are, I have to say, overwhelmingly of human origin. The remainder are the result of freak weather conditions known as mini-vortexes. Sorry Mr Rockefeller: give your money to charity instead.
David Humphrey, UK

Some of the formations are too perfect to be the work of pranksters. I do, however, think that they are the result of natural processes such as magnetic fields, underground archaeology or geology and the wind rather than aliens.
Barry Tregear, England

If aliens have the intelligence to get in and out of earth that many times without being seen, they could certainly come up with something better than a crop circle!
B. Kuzava, USA

Our planet is a marvellous wonder and has secrets that it will never reveal! Freak of nature or out of this world - who knows or ever will know!!
Cathie, England

Piffle. That these things could be anything but people playing the ignorant, superstitious and stupid for fools, is patently silly. If they were really the work of aliens, then what do they represent? A landing zone? How far up can one get above them before they can no longer be seen? Certainly not to the limits of the atmosphere. Are they simply an alien version of 'Kilroy was here?' The fact that

people waste more than a few seconds pondering this issue reinforces my faith in the basic stupidity of mankind.
Jim Hubbell, USA

I tend to have an open mind on most things and if you are inclined to think we are the only ones inhabiting this galaxy you are very naive. Of the 100 billion plus stars this side of the galactic centre, why should ours be the only one to have a rock with life attached floating around it. Also, alien intelligence is likely to be considerably more advanced than ours. Humans have been around for about 15 million years, a blink of an eye in the 5 billion years the Earth has.
I reckon any advanced alien race could warrant no real reason to spend their valuable time seriously interacting with us, like we don't really bother interacting much with say, ants or beetles. But there are some people that catalogue and monitor the progress of ants and beetles etc (why i don't know) so why not catalogue the Earth?
Mark, England

The formation of crop circles goes against all the rules of human logic. However, all you hoax theorists ask yourself this..... what are the rules of an aliens logic?
Paul Marshall, USA

If Crop Circles are made by aliens, it is unlikely that 90% of these are found in Britain. Unless somehow the aliens are extremely fond of Britain. I think Crop Circles are a chapter of "Dr. Who".
Thiam Huat, Singapore

A bunch of hippies with nothing else to do at night except ruin a proportion of farmers' crops, because they have no mates to meet at the pub.
Jonathan Harker, New Zealand

I don't think that the crop circles are a hoax. Some of them look a bit to complex to be manmade. Suppose that the crop circles were made by aliens, wouldn't that be great? A sign from outer space!
Gilbert Koningstein, The Netherlands

Crop circles could well be hoaxes, but shouldn't we investigate why people would want to create them in the first place? Could they be linked to Stonehenge, and what makes people sure that they are related to UFOs? Perhaps they (crop circles) are unmodified gateways between the reality of this universe and a parallel spiritual plain.

Mark Hampson, England

Always the rural folks cooking up such stories. Crop circles are the creation of bored farmers or bored citizens of small towns who are having a laugh at the expense of those fools called UFO enthusiasts. A counter question, if you wanted to communicate with someone far away, would you travel all that way to merely draw shapes in someone's back yard hoping someone would notice?

Steve Kenney, USA

Years ago in Minnesota, a UFO believer had a joke played on him by his brother-in-law. The in-law made circular burn marks in the man's cornfield. The UFO believer was ecstatic to find the discovery on his property. A few days later, the joker in law informed him it was a gag that he went to a great deal of trouble to play on him. No matter. The UFO believer still thought he had alien visitors. They are a stubborn breed, those UFO freaks.

David Hulbert, USA

The only reasonable argument for crop circles being of 'alien' construction would be that they only seem to appear in localised areas of the world in arable farmland. This, however is also the most convincing argument against the 'alien' theories, I mean, who has ever heard of a mud circle or a dust circle? This is either the work of intelligent life-forms, or people from Hampshire.

Lisa Harvey-Smith, England

So little green men are flying billions of miles in highly sophisticated craft simply in order to hide behind clouds and draw circles in cornfields near where hippies are squatting? Hmm ... maybe not.

Gretl Coudrille, UK

Maybe, maybe not there is no solid proof either way.
Efrem Gebrehiwet, Canada

Aliens? No. A Hoax? No. Natural phenomenon? Quite plausible.
There are many things we don't yet understand about this sphere
we live on. The corn lays undamaged facing the same way with no
footprints approaching the patterns. I doubt a hoaxer would be able
to create this effect with string and a plank of wood without
damaging the crop. This study should include a timed attempt at
creating these intricate circles using sting and planks of wood, and
see if they can achieve the same effect.
Michael, UK

Since these formations are only properly visible from the air, isn't
it obvious that it's not passing aliens signalling to us, but aliens
here on earth sending messages to their airborne brethren ? By a
stroke of luck, the peak foreign holiday season on Mars coincides
with the best growing season in Wiltshire.
Dave Smith, UK

Fake? What do you think? I can just imagine...somewhere on the
far side of the galaxy a race of aliens have spent vital resources and
years building a craft, and training their crew. Then travel in
suspended animation and suffer the perils of deep space, potential
super novae, black holes and worse, arrive on earth, 'draw' pretty
diagrams amongst plants - crop circles - and then, without a word
head back home. Mission accomplished. This is millennial
madness, and sadly the result of a post-Christian society looking to
the sky for a God-substitute.
Jon Gardner, England

Wouldn't it just be the most amazing thing to happen to us, if there
was something out there coming to visit us.
Shabaz Siddique, England

Clearly not many of these respondents have actually been in a crop
formation nor have they sought any information other than that
which is presented to them. Why do cameras and mobile phones
fail to operate in formations? Why do dogs often refuse to enter?
Why have some post-menopausal women started bleeding again?
Why do many people report dizziness and nausea, others elation

and peace? Why does lodging (aka. wind damage) show similar physical effects to those found in crops circles? Where are the photographs of hoaxers in mid-creation? Why haven't any been caught and prosecuted?
Damian Brothers, England

It is a sad reflection on mankind as we approach the new millennium that superstition and irrationality still guide the thought processes of so many people.
Richard Gibson, UK

Unexplained phenomenon are always a challenge to any people. Crop circles are not recent, but ancient, and clearly challenge explanation. No so-called hoaxers could do this. Let's hope the research scheduled this year will bring some new facts out!
Robert Heilman, USA

Of course they are fake. They are planted just like the cereal they are made in. How come few are caught doing it? Imagine: Helicopter dangling disc at end of a line. The spinning disc causes the effect of a circle in the crop. Helicopter goes away. Crop circle formed by "mysterious" craft!
Graham Roberts, UK

Just ask yourself one question, why would a species intelligent enough to cross vast distances of empty space land on a planet and make pretty circles in the fields of crops? Crop circles have always been the work of terrestrial beings armed with string, ladders, planks and sense of humour.
Ian Thomas, England

I believe they are a craze just as is graffiti.
Michael Smith, UK

I have seen many crop circles as I used to live in the Marlborough Downs where great many of the crop circles appeared in the early nineties. I can honestly say that the locals including the farmers are just as puzzled as everyone else. The things I remember are the fact the corn is not broken but bent over and still alive. Some of the crop circles were impossible to get to. Strange electromagnetic fields seem to be around some the crop circles and I remember TV

cameramen not being able to film the crop circles close up due to malfunctioning cameras.
Tim, England

Of course they're a hoax. It may be absurd to suggest we're the only intelligent life in the universe, but it's just as ludicrous to think that aliens would travel for centuries, millennia even, purely to mess around in our farms. Besides, I know someone who does it. Although his are frankly rubbish. But then, I'm not sure he isn't an alien anyhow.

Rob Marriott, UK

In my opinion crop circles are not a hoax, I base my theory on the fact that some of the circles that have been produced overnight both in the U.K and abroad are far too intricate in design to have been knocked up by someone with a torch and a lawn mower. At the end of the day I personally feel that people are experiencing a classic fear of the unknown and dealing with this by labelling these and other strange phenomena as the work of hoaxers when really they don't have a clue and this is the most convenient answer.
P.Fletcher, England

Of course they're a hoax - the hoaxers have put their hands up! The persistence of this kind of new age thinking in the face of all the evidence including the confessions of those responsible is more worthy of research than are crop circles.
Paul Cooper, UK

How about putting one in for the Turner prize? There's no doubt they are of human origin and it's no more dotty that wearing strange hats crossing London Bridge last May 'for art'.
K. Jackson, USA

Judging from the amount and frequency of these 'phenomena' I believe it seems rather too much like hard work to be a hoax. But to suggest the involvement of extra-terrestrial life is far-fetched. This money would be better spent investigating whether Scottish football referees are in fact aliens.
Gus McGhee, Germany

It would be rather depressing to think that after the vast expense and time it would take to reach our planet that all the 'visitors' wished to do was vandalise a few crops!! Plus, how come we don't get similar patterns appearing on snow?
John Wedderburn, UK

When crops are given too much fertiliser, they become too top heavy and are easily blown over by the wind. If you were to add fertiliser to the ground before planting in a 'crop circle' pattern, when it grows the pattern will emerge as the areas of fallen crops.
Colin Harrison, UK

Hoax? No way! Even on the picture on the top of this page you can see that they are real and created with techniques we have absolutely no idea of. Besides all of these marks have meanings. This one shows Earth and Moon. Earth is the third planet from the sun and we can see that Earth symbol is marked with 3 vertical lines aside. Moon is the only Earth's satellite and we can see that Moon sign is marked with 1 vertical line. Besides, Earth and Moon proportions showed by these signs match real ones. It's a disputable question who creates these marks. But one can be said for sure: no one on Earth can do this so precisely.
Alex Wierzbowsky, EU

There are no aliens and there are no UFO's and all this is just a hoax. (what most people who believe in UFO's do not realise that even if there were space travellers, they could not get here as they would be too far away to find us.)
And also probably we are the only intelligent life form anywhere in the universe. Even it there is life of any kind in our galaxy, or any galaxy, it is so far away, that we are never going to find it, or know about it. Yes, we are alone!!!
Marius Balogh, Australia

They're either a hoax of an earthly nature or there are some very bored ET's out there having a joke at our expense!
Guy Dawson, UK

The whole 'crop circles are formed by aliens' malarkey is a swizz. Quite honestly, I think people believing in extra-terrestrial activity

in cornfields are quite mad. Wheat, fields on the other hand...
Rupert C Kent, London, UK

Crop circles definitely exist. My garden backs onto a large field of barley. One morning, many many moons ago I awoke to find the local farmer scratching his head and chewing his corn in a very perplexed manner. When I enquired as to his confusion he told me to go upstairs and gaze over his field. I did this and low and behold there was a perfect circle of flattened barley in the middle of the field.
Naturally I expected tom foolery from the local ruffians but when he pointed out that there were marks leading into the field, I had to scratch my head in amazement too. There had been many strange goings on in the hamlet round then, only that night had a large helicopter landed in the field!!!
Michael Norton, England

Of course Corn Circles are fake! But that is not the issue - the issue is why do so many people believe that aliens could be responsible? It appears to me that these people believe in a whole load of twaddle - all this 'New Age' nonsense - probably something to do with the breakdown of ordered religion for many people in this country - they're searching for some spiritual fulfilment. Well, they won't find it in a field full if hippies off the M4!
They need a cold shower!
Charles Ungard, UK

Although some corn-circles are certainly hoaxes, the sites that are confirmed as being made by humans tend to be rather simplistic, tatty affairs, quite unlike the geometric precision and beauty found in some examples. There is no way that these are produced by hoaxers.
I don't believe aliens have anything to do with it either and I personally support the freak weather conditions or natural phenomenon explanations but I hope that this new study can provide some definite proof.
Dave Cogbill, UK

Either a hoax or demonic activity!
E.W. Dunn UK

There is no hoax. Nor is there any indication that they are anything other than natural phenomena.
Daryle Denomy, Canada

So we get crop circles but no desert circles, forest circles, pasture circles, pebble circles - I would expect the superior beings who are our alleged visitors to do something a little more impressive than flatten down a bit of corn.
Maybe they just wanted to freak out the farmers, or perhaps writing any of the extremely basic languages used to communicate on this planet is beyond them??
Long may crop circles continue if it means more Yankee dollars coming our way!
Richard, UK

The public seem to be very misinformed about crop circles in general. The BBC Country File program did nothing that wasn't already known about the phenomenon. What they failed to show after the circles had been made was the broken stems that were strewn over all the formations, something that is not seen in many of the others.
Crop circle investigators have been asked to prove that they are genuine. The so-called "crop circle artists", "hoaxers", etc have never been asked to provide evidence of which formations they have made. Based on this I can claim to have made every circle in the world.
As for Laurance Rockefeller funding research. Who are his scientists? Where are they from? There is a lack of basic investigation from croppies and media alike.
Mark Haywood UK

High numbers of Young Farmers equals high numbers of crop circles, I think there is a connection.
M. Gallacher, Scotland

Hmm... If those circles were a hoax, then how come their creators have not been caught on a single occasion, in a relatively dense populated island, such as Britain?
I believe that human mind alone cannot be so creative... until it's exposed to AN EXAMPLE, and then just modifies it and simulates. My opinion, reasoning from the info I got so far, those

circles are indeed something of "outer" nature.
Alex "Sasha", Russia

Since the men responsible for the whole hoax have already come
forward and flawlessly reproduced the crop circles, this seems like
a moot point. But then people generally don't like their beliefs
questioned, so I'm not surprised that the debate still lingers.
Croppists are looking for ways to explain an existing belief; they
should instead be looking at beliefs to explain existing facts. But
how often does that happen?
Kat, USA

Perhaps crop circles are the work of inter-galactic graffiti artists.
Translated they probably say 'Zog Was Here'.
Phil Huddlestone, UK

The most noticeable thing about the current wave of crop circles is
how close many of them are to tourist sites like Avebury and
Glastonbury - just what you need to get a good hoax noticed!
Of course, the New Agers claim this is due to the 'mystical power'
of such sites, but I prefer the simpler explanation that people like
their work to get attention.
James W Bottomley, UK

A few friends and myself created a circle one night. The resulting
investigation by UFO "experts" showed strange radiation readings
and psychic vibes in the centre of the circle. It just shows how
stupid some people are.
Joe, England

Has anyone ever been caught making a crop formation? No.
Wiltshire is not the back of beyond. Whilst there is no doubt that
many formations, in this country at least are manmade, this does
not explain the 10,000 plus formations that have appeared in India
in the last twenty years, many of them in remote fields far away
from media cameras and tourists.
Neill Wood, UK

How many of the hoaxers must confess before it is accepted that
they are a hoax? Why do so many people insist that there be proof
that flying saucers don't exist? Accept the evidence (the

confessions) and let the rest of us get on with our lives.
Richard T. Ketchum, USA

While I generally approve of seriously-minded scientific investigation of unexplained phenomena - after all, lightning bolts were supposed to be all sorts of paranormal things until Benjamin Franklin put his mind to work - I can't help feeling that crop circles hold no great discovery for mankind. Except, perhaps, that some forms of graffiti are much more imaginative than others.
M. Reed Austin, UK

I am a tax advisor and drink shandy. Only when me and my advisor chums have had too little lemonade in our shandies and get a little boisterous do we go out and try and make crop circles. Unfortunately they are usually crop squiggles.
Steve McMullen, England

Hasn't anyone else noticed that the first link site is by the circle makers themselves?
David, UK

Hail fellow Kights! Crop circles are the work of my teams of Pixie Knights in their relentless pursuit of Pixie Magic.
King Arthur of Camalot, England

Crop Circles are by far the most interesting mystery of the 20th century. We have more or less successfully debunked Nessie and Bigfoot and all that rubbish, crop circles are still, unexplained for the most part.
They happen in too many places, too often, for even a fairly well organised group of persons would be hard pressed not to EVER get caught.
Crop Circles are scary, they are unknown, that is why most of the people here are moved to write, and to assert they 'do not exist'.
Roger, USA

I am 74 years old and can remember crop circles in cornfields from when I was a child living first in Norfolk and later in Dorset. Some of them were quite elaborate. The country people accepted them, they were part of the landscape, and had been for generations.
There was no talk of them being hoaxed in those days, people were

much more law abiding, and the thought of deliberately damaging a farmer's crop was unthinkable.
I have always believed a proportion of the formations are real.
Sam Dalston, UK

Anybody who takes a step back to consider this 'phenomenon' realises that aliens, or any other alternative explanation just does not hold up. Even a die hard believer forced to answer why the aliens have targeted corn fields of all places, and why these bizarre patterns have been the result of technology far beyond us usually concedes the point.
Other forms of intelligence are very likely to exist - but get real. Corn circles have nothing whatsoever to do with that issue.
Chafir, England

I've seen a few circles from the air myself. All were connected to a road or track, either by tractor ruts or a direct path in the crops in some cases! Is this proof that aliens walk?
The real mystery is why people prefer to believe their own fantasies, rather than testimony and demonstrations from the hoaxers.
Then again, some people believe that Eastenders is a fly-on-the-wall documentary!
Rik Alewijnse, UK

Crop circle tours are selling out? A US billionaire is financing an investigation? Sounds like a money maker to me.
Tim Donovan, US

Printed in Great Britain
by Amazon